KANSAS CITY
ROYALS

STARS, STATS, HISTORY, AND MORE!

BY K. C. KELLEY

Published by The Child's World®
1980 Lookout Drive • Mankato, MN 56003-1705
800-599-READ • www.childsworld.com

ISBN 9781503828254
LCCN 2018944838

Printed in the United States of America
PA02392

Photo Credits:
Cover: Joe Robbins (2).
Interior: AP Images: 9, Charlie Riedel 10, Cliff Schiappa
17; Dreamstime.com: Ffooter 13, Jerry Coli 29; Newscom:
Adam Bowl/Icon SW 5; Nick Wosicka/Icon SW 19;
Scott Winston/Icon SMI 27; Joe Robbins 6;
Joe Robbins: 14, 20, 23, 24.

About the Author

K.C. Kelley is a huge sports
fan who has written more
than 100 books for kids. His
favorite sport is baseball.
He has also written about
football, basketball, soccer,
and even auto racing! He lives
in Santa Barbara, California.

On the Cover

Main photo: Catcher
Salvador Perez
Inset: Hall of Fame hitter
George Brett

CONTENTS

GO, ROYALS!

he Kansas City Royals went a long time between championships. Their fans thought it was worth the wait! Happy Royals fans celebrated in 2015 when their team took the top trophy. Now they want to get another one! Let's meet the Royals!

Infielder Whit Merrifield hopes to bring another title to Kansas City. ➤

WHO ARE THE ROYALS?

ansas City plays in the American League (AL). That group is part of Major League Baseball (MLB). MLB also includes the National League (NL). There are 30 teams in MLB. The winner of the AL plays the winner of the NL in the **World Series**.

◄ *Alex Gordon has been slugging for the Royals since 2007.*

WHERE THEY CAME FROM

In 1969, MLB added four new teams. They were known as **expansion** teams. The Royals were one of two new AL teams. (The other was the Seattle Pilots. That team later became the Milwaukee Brewers!) The Royals have stayed in the same place since 1969. Believe it or not, the team is named for cows. The American Royal breed is popular in Missouri. Kansas City is home to a show featuring those cows each year!

Amos Otis joined Kansas City in 1970 and played there for 14 seasons. ➤

WHO THEY PLAY

The Royals play in the AL Central Division. The other teams in the AL Central are the Chicago White Sox, the Cleveland Indians, the Detroit Tigers, and the Minnesota Twins. The Royals play more games against their division **rivals** than against other teams. In all, the Royals play 162 games each season. They play 81 games at home and 81 on the road. Kansas City sometimes plays its Missouri rival, the St. Louis Cardinals of the NL.

◄ *Whit Merrifield tags out the Cardinals Jedd Gyorko in a game between Missouri teams.*

WHERE THEY PLAY

Royals Stadium opened in 1973. For many years, it was one of the few in MLB that had **artificial turf**. Fans and players love the huge water fountain in centerfield. When the Royals score, jets of water shoot up. Kansas City itself is known for its many fountains around town. In 1993, the ballpark got a new name. Kauffman Stadium was named for the team's longtime owner, Ewing Kauffman.

Huge sprays of water fly out of the Kauffman Stadium fountains. ➤

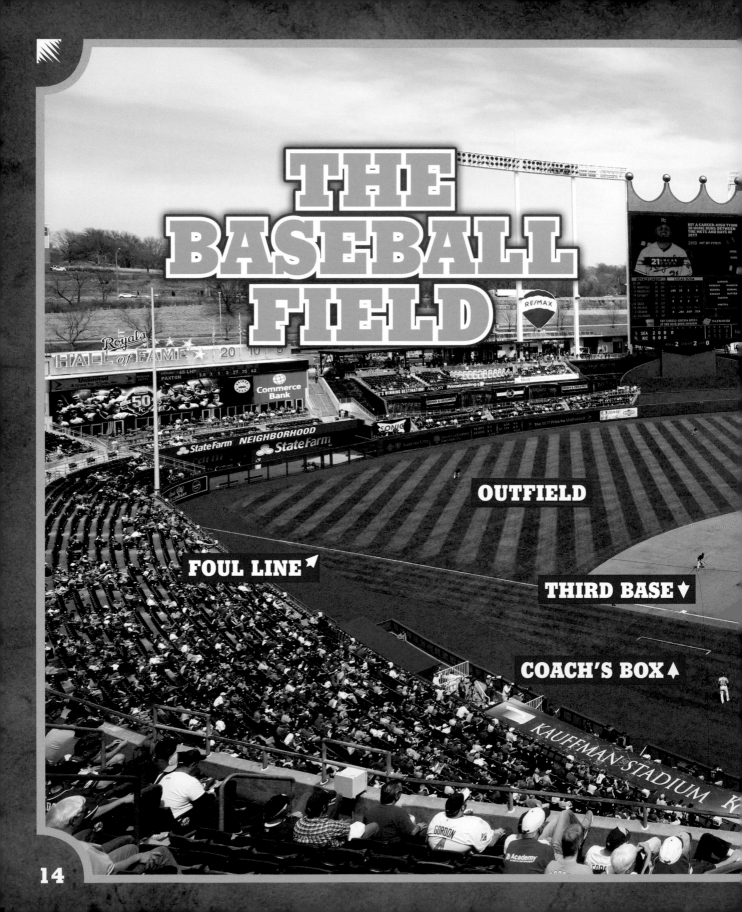

THE BASEBALL FIELD

OUTFIELD

FOUL LINE

THIRD BASE

COACH'S BOX

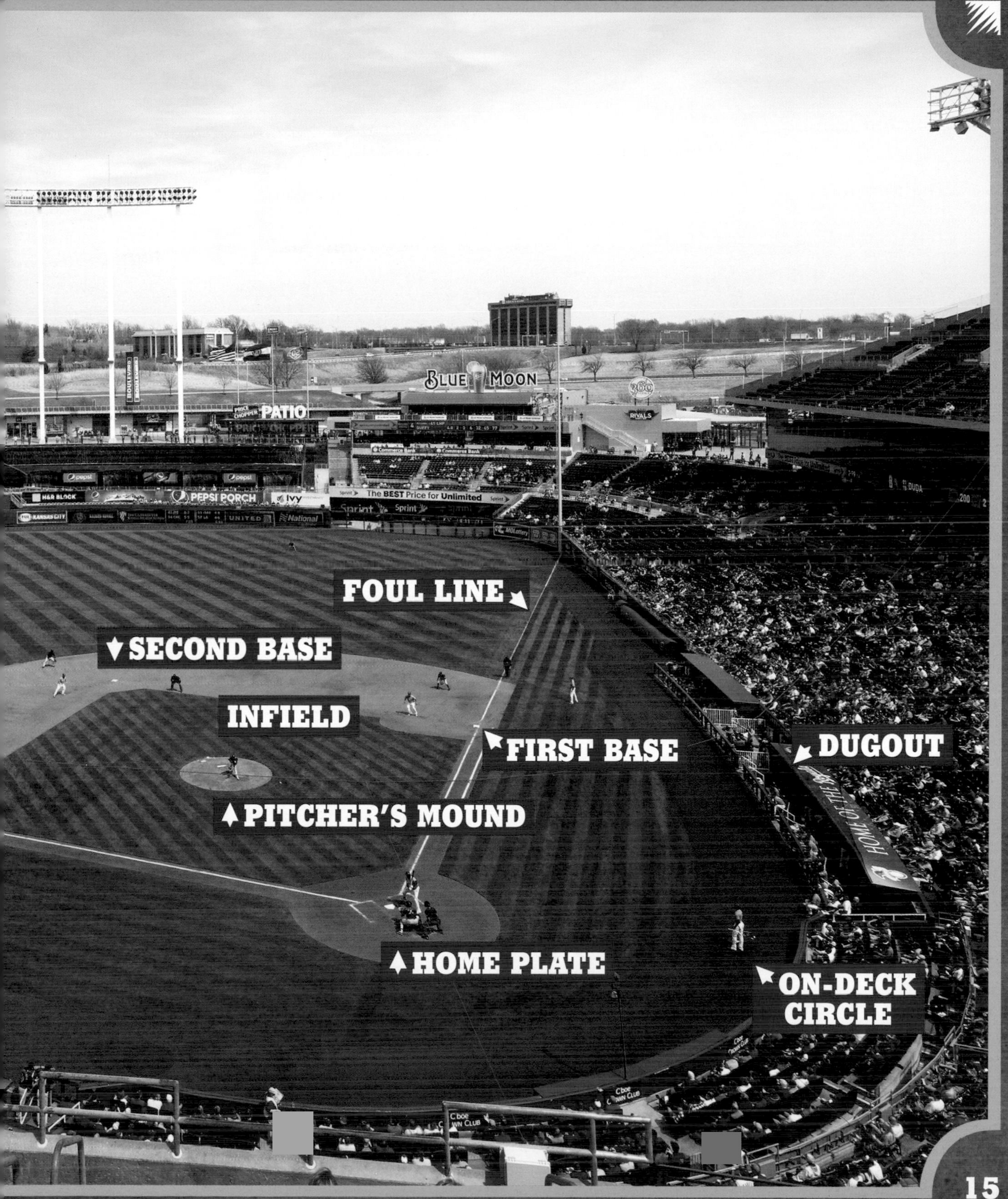

FOUL LINE ▼

▼ SECOND BASE

INFIELD

◄ FIRST BASE

DUGOUT ◄

▲ PITCHER'S MOUND

▲ HOME PLATE

◄ ON-DECK CIRCLE

BIG DAYS

The Royals have had a lot of great days in their history. Here are a few of them.

1976—In the Royals' eighth season, they won their first division title. They were part of the AL West at the time.

1985—Kansas City won its first World Series. Pitcher Bret Saberhagen won two games. He allowed only one run in 18 innings.

2015—Back on top! After 30 long years, the Royals won an exciting World Series. They beat the New York Mets.

Bret Saberhagen (31) led the Royals to the 1985 title. ➤

TOUGH DAYS

**L**ike every team, the Royals have had some not-so-great days, too. Here are a few their fans might not want to recall.

1992—Talk about a tough start! The Royals won only one of their first 17 games!

2005—The Royals lost a team-record 106 games. They even tried three different **managers**! None of the managers worked out. The season included a 19-game losing streak.

2017—The Royals still had hopes of a playoff spot. Those hopes mostly vanished after a game in September. Minnesota beat Kansas City 17–0. It was the worst shutout loss in Royals history.

▼ *Royals manager Ned Yost probably wanted to be alone. He was watching his team lose 17–0 in 2017.*

MEET THE FANS!

Royals fans loved it when their team started in Kansas City. They have stayed loyal ever since. The team has rewarded them with some exciting seasons. At the ballpark, Sluggerrr helps the fans cheer. He's a lion wearing a royal crown!

◄ *Why all the "r's" in this mascot's name? It's a lion and it's roaring!*

HEROES THEN

or a young team, the Royals have had a lot of big stars. Hall of Famer George Brett is one of the best third basemen ever. He had a great **batting average** and 3,154 hits. Frank White played steady second base for many years. He had more than 2,000 hits. Amos Otis was a fan favorite. He was a speedy outfielder for 14 seasons. Pitcher Bret Saberhagen won the **Cy Young Award** twice with the Royals.

George Brett was known for his bat and for his all-out playing style. ➤

HEROES NOW

atcher Salvador Pérez is the Royals leader. He helped the team win the 2015 World Series. Alex Gordon is a top defensive outfielder. Young Whit Merrifield steals a lot of bases. The pitching staff is led by righthander Danny Duffy.

◄ *Salvador Pérez has been a six-time All-Star for the Royals.*

GEARING UP

aseball players wear team uniforms. On defense, they wear leather gloves to catch the ball. As batters, they wear hard helmets. This protects them from pitches. Batters hit the ball with long wood bats. Each player chooses his own size of bat. Catchers have the toughest job. They wear a lot of protection.

THE BASEBALL

The outside of the Major League baseball is made from cow leather. Two leather pieces shaped like 8s are stitched together. There are 108 stitches of red thread. These stitches help players grip the ball. Inside, the ball has a small center of cork and rubber. Hundreds of feet of yarn are tightly wound around this center.

◄ CATCHER'S MASK AND HELMET

WRIST BANDS ►

CHEST PROTECTOR ►

◄ CATCHER'S MITT

SHIN GUARDS ►

CATCHER'S GEAR

TEAM STATS

Here are some of the all-time career records for the Kansas City Royals. All these stats are through the 2018 regular season.

HOME RUNS	
George Brett	317
Mike Sweeney	197

RBI	
George Brett	1,596
Hal McRae	1,012

BATTING AVERAGE	
Jose Offerman	.306
George Brett	.305

STOLEN BASES	
Willie Wilson	612
Amos Otis	340

WINS	
Paul Splittorff	166
Dennis Leonard	144

STRIKEOUTS	
Kevin Appier	1,458
Mark Gubicza	1,366

Jeff Montgomery was one of the top relief pitchers of the 1990s. ➤

SAVES	
Jeff Montgomery	304
Dan Quisenberry	238

GLOSSARY

artificial turf (AR-tuh-FISH-ul TURF) plastic material used instead of real grass

batting average (BAT-ing AV-rij) a measure of how often a player gets a base hit

Cy Young Award (SY YUNG uh-WARD) an honor given to the top pitcher in each league

expansion (ex-PAN-shun) in baseball, when new teams are added to a league

manager (MAN-uh-jir) a person who runs a baseball team, choosing the lineup and pitchers

rivals (RYE-vuhlz) two people or groups competing for the same thing

World Series (WURLD SEE-reez) the annual championship of Major League Baseball

IN THE LIBRARY

Connery-Boyd, Peg. *Kansas City Royals: Big Book of Activities*. Chicago, IL: Sourcebooks/Jabberwocky, 2016.

Rhodes, Sam. *Kansas City Royals (Inside MLB)*. Calgary, AB: Weigl, 2018.

Sports Illustrated Kids (editors). *Big Book of Who: Baseball*. New York, NY: Sports Illustrated Kids, 2017.

ON THE WEB

Visit our website for links about the Kansas City Royals:
childsworld.com/links

Note to Parents, Teachers, and Librarians: We routinely verify our web links to make sure they are safe and active sites. So encourage your readers to check them out!

INDEX

5/19